CW00704300

Parenting with Calm and Compassion

Mastering Anger for a Harmonious Home

Rhea Menzie

ANGER MANAGEMENT FOR PARENTS
© Copyright 2023 by Rhea Menzie
All rights reserved

This document is geared towards providing exact and reliable information with regards to the topic and issue covered. The publication is sold with the idea that the publisher is not required to render accounting, officially permitted, or otherwise, qualified services. If advice is necessary, legal or professional, a practiced individual in the profession should be ordered.

From a Declaration of Principles which was accepted and approved equally by a Committee of the American Bar Association and a Committee of Publishers and Associations.

In no way is it legal to reproduce, duplicate, or transmit any part of this document in either electronic means or in printed format. Recording of this publication is strictly prohibited and any storage of this document is not allowed unless with written permission from the publisher. All rights reserved.

The information provided herein is stated to be truthful and consistent, in that any liability, in terms of inattention or otherwise, by any usage or abuse of any policies, processes, or directions contained within is the solitary and utter responsibility of the recipient reader. Under no circumstances will any legal responsibility or blame be held against the publisher for any reparation, damages, or monetary loss due to the information herein, either directly or indirectly.

Respective authors own all copyrights not held by the publisher.

The information herein is offered for informational purposes solely, and is universal as so. The presentation of the information is without contract or any type of guarantee assurance.

The trademarks that are used are without any consent, and the publication of the trademark is without permission or backing by the trademark owner. All trademarks and brands within this book are for clarifying purposes only and are owned by the owners themselves, not affiliated with this document.

TABLE OF CONTENTS

Chapter 1: Understanding Anger

Parenthood is a profound and rewarding journey filled with moments of joy, love, and connection. It's a journey that offers us the opportunity to nurture and guide the next generation, watching them grow, learn, and flourish. However, alongside these moments of immense happiness, parenthood can also present its fair share of challenges and frustrations.

Anger is a universal human emotion, and as parents, we are not exempt from experiencing it. In fact, parenting can be a fertile ground for the emergence of anger due to the myriad responsibilities, pressures, and expectations that come with raising children. From sleepless nights with a crying infant to the trials and tribulations of the teenage years, parenting is a complex and emotionally charged endeavor.

This book, "Anger Management for Parents," is a compassionate guide for mothers and fathers alike who find themselves wrestling with the powerful and often overwhelming emotion of anger. We recognize that anger is a natural response to the stressors of parenthood, and our aim is not to deny or suppress it, but rather to help you understand and manage it constructively.

The Nature of Anger

Anger is a primal emotion, deeply rooted in our evolutionary history. It is our body's response to a perceived threat or injustice, triggering a cascade of physiological and psychological changes. When we feel anger, our heart rate increases, our muscles tense, and our minds race with thoughts of frustration, irritation, or even rage.

In the context of parenting, anger can arise from a multitude of situations. It might be ignited by a child's persistent misbehavior, a teenager's defiance, or simply the unrelenting demands of parenthood. Regardless of the trigger, anger is a signal that something is amiss, and it calls for our attention.

The Impact of Anger on Parenting

While anger itself is a normal and healthy emotion, how we choose to express and manage it as parents is of paramount importance. Uncontrolled or destructive anger can have far-reaching and detrimental effects on our lives and the lives of our children.

When anger is unbridled, it can harm the parent-child relationship, erode trust, and create an atmosphere of fear or tension in the home. Children, even at a young age, are highly perceptive and sensitive to their parents' emotional states. Chronic parental anger can lead to children developing their own emotional and behavioral challenges.

Recognizing Your Triggers

Each one of us has our unique set of triggers—those circumstances or behaviors that activate our anger. These triggers often have deep roots, stemming from our own childhood experiences, personal values, and the current stresses we face. By identifying and understanding our triggers, we gain insight into the patterns of our anger and can begin to address them.

Through self-awareness and introspection, we can recognize when our anger is building and take steps to intervene before it escalates into a destructive force. This book will provide you with the tools and strategies to better understand and manage your anger, helping you foster a more peaceful and harmonious family life.

In the chapters that follow, we will explore various aspects of anger management for parents, from the effects of anger on children to techniques for calming down in the heat of the moment. Our goal is to empower you to become the parent you aspire to be—one who models emotional intelligence, resilience, and constructive ways of handling anger.

CHAPTER 2: THE EFFECTS OF ANGER ON CHILDREN

In the intricate dance of parenting, emotions often take center stage. Anger, with its fiery intensity, can cast a long shadow, affecting not only parents but also their children. In this chapter, we delve deeper into the profound impact of parental anger on children's emotional well-being and the long-term consequences it can bear.

How Anger Affects Children's Emotional Well-being

Children are like sponges, absorbing not only the knowledge and values their parents impart but also the emotional climate of their home. When parental anger becomes a frequent guest in their lives, it can cast a heavy cloud over their emotional well-being. Anxiety, fear, and insecurity may take root, affecting their overall happiness.

Expanding our understanding, we acknowledge that children may internalize their parents' anger, believing it to be a reflection of their own shortcomings. This self-blame can damage their self-esteem and lead to a profound sense of inadequacy.

Long-Term Consequences of Parental Anger

As parents, we strive to provide a nurturing environment that fosters our children's growth. However, unchecked anger can lead to unintended consequences. The seeds of resentment and confusion sown during childhood can sprout into more profound issues in adolescence and adulthood.

In this section, we explore the potential long-term effects of parental anger. From difficulties in forming healthy relationships to struggles with self-regulation, the ramifications of early exposure to anger can be far-reaching. By understanding these potential consequences, parents can be motivated to address their anger and create a more harmonious family environment.

Signs Your Child May Be Affected by Your Anger

Recognizing the impact of parental anger on children is essential, but equally vital is the ability to identify the signs that your child may be affected. Children often lack the vocabulary to express their emotions fully, making it imperative for parents to be attuned to subtle indicators.

We delve into these signs, shedding light on behavioral changes, emotional shifts, and communication patterns that may signal your child's struggle with the effects of parental anger. Understanding these signs equips parents with the knowledge they need to intervene and create a safer emotional space for their children.

By expanding our comprehension of how parental anger affects children, we pave the way for a more empathetic and nurturing approach to parenting.

CHAPTER 3: THE POWER OF SELF-AWARENESS

As parents, it's easy to become entangled in the daily whirlwind of responsibilities, emotions, and challenges that come with raising children. In this chapter, we explore the vital role that self-awareness plays in managing and mitigating parental anger. Self-awareness is the cornerstone of change, and by developing a deeper understanding of our thoughts, emotions, and behaviors, we can take meaningful steps towards a more peaceful and harmonious family life.

The Importance of Self-Reflection

Self-reflection is the practice of turning our attention inward and examining our thoughts, feelings, and actions. In the context of anger management for parents, self-reflection serves several critical purposes:

Recognizing Triggers: Self-reflection helps us identify the specific situations, events, or behaviors that trigger our anger. By understanding our triggers, we can anticipate them and prepare ourselves to respond differently.

Understanding Underlying Emotions: Beneath anger often lies a more nuanced web of emotions, such as frustration, fear, or sadness. Self-reflection enables us to uncover these underlying feelings and address them directly.

Connecting with Empathy: When we reflect on our own experiences, it becomes easier to empathize with our children's emotions and perspectives. This connection can facilitate more compassionate responses.

Evaluating Our Responses: Self-reflection allows us to evaluate our reactions to anger. Were our responses effective? Did they align with our values and parenting goals? What could we have done differently?

Identifying Your Anger Patterns

Anger often follows distinct patterns, both in terms of triggers and responses. By identifying these patterns, we gain valuable insights into our anger and can work towards more constructive responses:

Behavioral Patterns: Do you tend to shout, withdraw, or become physically aggressive when angry? Identifying your behavioral patterns helps you understand how you express anger.

Cognitive Patterns: What thoughts race through your mind when anger arises? Are there recurring beliefs or assumptions that fuel your anger? Identifying cognitive patterns is crucial for changing your thought processes.

Physical Patterns: Pay attention to the physical sensations that accompany your anger. Does your heart race? Do you clench your fists or jaw? Recognizing these physical cues can serve as early warnings.

Environmental Patterns: Are there specific environments or circumstances in which you are more prone to anger? Understanding these patterns can help you proactively manage anger triggers.

Tracking Your Emotional Responses

Emotions are complex, and anger is often a surface-level expression of deeper emotional states. Tracking your emotional responses involves:

Emotion Identification: When you feel anger rising, take a moment to identify the specific emotions you're experiencing. Are you feeling overwhelmed, anxious, or hurt? Acknowledging these emotions is the first step toward managing them.

Emotion Intensity: Rate the intensity of your emotions on a scale from 1 to 10. This can help you gauge the severity of your emotional reaction and track changes over time.

Emotion Duration: How long do your intense emotions persist? Some emotions may be fleeting, while others linger. Monitoring duration provides insights into emotional resilience.

Emotion Triggers: Take note of what triggered your emotional response. Was it a specific event, interaction, or thought? Identifying triggers aids in prevention and mitigation.

Self-awareness is an ongoing practice that requires dedication and patience. It's not about self-criticism but about understanding and accepting yourself more fully. As you delve deeper into self-reflection, recognize that change takes time, and setbacks are part of the journey. In the chapters that follow, we will explore practical techniques and exercises to enhance your self-awareness and harness its power in managing parental anger.

CHAPTER 4: MANAGING ANGER IN THE HEAT OF THE MOMENT

Parenting is filled with moments that test our patience and provoke our anger. In the thick of these challenging moments, it can be challenging to stay calm and composed. In this chapter, we delve into practical techniques and strategies for managing anger in the heat of the moment, allowing you to respond thoughtfully rather than react impulsively.

Techniques for Calming Down Quickly

- The Pause Button: When you feel anger rising, give yourself permission to pause. This simple act of stepping back mentally for a moment can help you avoid reacting impulsively. Use this time to collect your thoughts and emotions.

- Count to Ten: The age-old advice of counting to ten has a basis in psychology. Counting can redirect your focus away from anger and give your rational mind a chance to reassert itself.

- Visualization: Imagine a serene and calming place, whether it's a peaceful beach or a tranquil forest. Visualizing this safe haven can help reduce anger and stress in the moment.

- Positive Affirmations: Develop a set of positive affirmations that resonate with you. When anger flares, recite these affirmations to yourself. They can help reframe your thoughts and emotions.

Deep Breathing and Mindfulness Exercises

Deep belly breathing and mindfulness exercises are indispensable tools in the arsenal of anger management. Let's explore these techniques in more depth, providing you with a comprehensive understanding of their benefits and how to integrate them seamlessly into your life.

Deep Belly Breathing: A Calming Oasis

Deep breathing is a soothing balm for the agitated mind and body. It's a practice that harmonizes your physiological responses, counteracting the adrenaline surge that often accompanies anger. To maximize its effectiveness, let's expand on the technique:

Begin by finding a quiet, comfortable space where you won't be disturbed. Sit or lie down, whichever feels more relaxing for you. Close your eyes to enhance your inner focus.

Inhale deeply through your nose, allowing your abdomen to expand fully as you fill your lungs. Feel the gentle rise of your diaphragm as it pushes against your abdominal wall.

Pause for a moment, savoring the sensation of fullness.

Exhale slowly and completely through your mouth, feeling the release of tension and negativity with each outward breath.

Repeat this cycle several times, with each breath carrying away a bit more of the anger and frustration. Allow yourself to be fully present in this meditative state, letting go of racing thoughts and worries.

By expanding on this technique, you can create a ritual of deep belly breathing that becomes your sanctuary, a place of calm and tranquility in the midst of life's storms.

Mindful Awareness: Anchoring in the Present

Mindfulness is the practice of being fully present in the current moment, and it's a skill that can be a game-changer in anger management. It allows you to step out of the whirlwind of emotions and observe them without judgment. Here's how to deepen your mindfulness practice:

Find a quiet and comfortable space, just as you would for deep breathing. Close your eyes to minimize distractions.

Begin by paying attention to your breath. Notice the sensation of the air entering and leaving your nostrils or the rise and fall of your chest or abdomen.

Expand your awareness to your body. Scan from head to toe, noting any areas of tension or discomfort. With each breath, imagine releasing these tensions.

Now, broaden your awareness to your immediate surroundings. Listen to the sounds around you—the gentle hum of appliances, the distant traffic, or the rustling of leaves. Feel the texture of the surface you're sitting or lying on.

When thoughts or emotions arise (as they inevitably will), observe them without judgment, as if you're watching clouds pass by in the sky. Then gently return your focus to your breath and your surroundings.

Mindfulness is a practice that cultivates your ability to detach from strong emotions, preventing them from spiraling out of control. It's like creating a serene island within the tempestuous sea of anger.

Progressive Muscle Relaxation: Releasing Tension from Within

Progressive muscle relaxation is a body-centered technique that enhances your self-awareness and helps release physical tension—a common accompaniment to anger. Expanding on this technique:

Find your quiet and comfortable space. You know the drill—close your eyes, and let's begin.

Start at your toes. Tense the muscles in your toes for a few seconds, and then release. Feel the difference between tension and relaxation.

Move up to your calves and repeat the process. Then proceed to your thighs, buttocks, abdomen, chest, back, shoulders, arms, and neck. With each muscle group, tense and then release, allowing a wave of relaxation to wash over you.

As you release the tension in each muscle group, visualize the stress and anger dissipating from your body, leaving you feeling lighter and more at ease.

Progressive muscle relaxation not only relieves physical tension but also sends a signal to your mind that it's time to let go of anger. This technique helps bridge the gap between the physical and emotional aspects of anger management.

Guided Meditation: A Compass in the Storm

Guided meditation can be your trusted companion in times of anger and stress. It provides a structured path to relaxation and anger reduction. Here's how to make the most of it:

Find a quiet and comfortable space—yes, the familiar drill applies. Sit or lie down, and close your eyes.

Choose a guided meditation recording or app that aligns with your specific needs. Whether it's a meditation focused on releasing anger, cultivating patience, or finding inner peace, there's a wealth of resources available.

Follow the guidance of the meditation, allowing the soothing voice to lead you through a journey of calmness and emotional release.

Guided meditation offers a structured and supportive way to manage anger when it feels overwhelming. It's like having a wise friend by your side, gently leading you toward serenity.

By expanding on these techniques, you create a robust toolbox for managing anger effectively and nurturing emotional well-being. These practices can become more than just strategies; they can become a way of life, enriching your days with tranquility and balance.

Using Time-Outs Effectively

- The Time-Out Chair: Time-outs aren't just for children. If you feel anger escalating and fear that you might say or do something hurtful, excuse yourself from the situation temporarily. Use this time to regain composure and perspective.

- Communicate Your Need for a Break: If possible, communicate to your child that you need a break to cool down. Let them know that it's not a punishment but a way to ensure a healthier interaction later.

- Set Boundaries: Establish a designated time-out space where you can go to decompress. This can be a quiet corner, a comfortable chair, or even your bedroom.

- Reflect and Regroup: During your time-out, reflect on the source of your anger, your emotional response, and alternative ways to handle the situation. Write down your thoughts and feelings in a journal if it helps.

Managing anger in the heat of the moment is an essential skill for parents. It allows you to model emotional regulation for your children and foster a more peaceful home environment. These techniques and exercises are not only practical but can also become integral parts of your daily life, helping you respond to challenging moments with grace and resilience. In the chapters that follow, we will continue to explore strategies for nurturing a healthier relationship with anger as a parent.

CHAPTER 5: COMMUNICATION SKILLS FOR DIFFUSING ANGER

Effective communication is the cornerstone of healthy relationships, and this holds especially true in the context of parenting. In this chapter, we delve into essential communication skills that can help you defuse anger, create understanding, and build stronger connections with your children.

Effective Listening and Empathy

Active Listening: Active listening involves giving your full attention to your child when they express their thoughts, feelings, or concerns. Maintain eye contact, nod in acknowledgment, and use verbal cues like "I see" or "Tell me more." This shows your child that you value their perspective.

Validation: Validating your child's emotions means acknowledging their feelings without judgment. Phrases like "I understand why you're upset" or "It's okay to feel that way" convey empathy and support.

Reflective Listening: Reflective listening involves paraphrasing what your child has said to ensure you've understood correctly. For example, you might say, "So, you're feeling frustrated because your friend didn't want to play with you today. Is that right?"

Empathetic Responses: Put yourself in your child's shoes and try to imagine how they might be feeling. Respond with empathy by saying things like, "I can imagine that must have been really disappointing."

Assertive Communication

"I" Statements: Instead of using accusatory language, express your feelings using "I" statements. For instance, instead of saying, "You always leave your toys out, and it's so annoying!" you could say, "I feel frustrated when I see toys left out because it makes our home cluttered."

Expressing Boundaries: Clearly communicate your boundaries and expectations to your child. Be firm but respectful in asserting your limits. For example, "In our family, we don't raise our voices when we're upset. Let's find a calm way to talk about this."

Active Problem-Solving: Encourage open dialogue and active problem-solving. When conflicts arise, involve your child in finding solutions. This fosters a sense of responsibility and collaboration.

Conflict Resolution Strategies

Cooling-Off Periods: When tensions are high, suggest taking a short break to cool off. This can be a mutual agreement with your child to revisit the issue later when both of you are calmer.

Negotiation and Compromise: Teach your child the art of negotiation and compromise. Discuss how both parties can make concessions to reach a mutually satisfying solution.

Use of "I" Statements in Conflict: Encourage your child to express their feelings using "I" statements when they have conflicts with others. This helps them communicate their needs and emotions assertively.

Model Conflict Resolution: Model healthy conflict resolution in your interactions with your child and with others. Children learn by observing, so demonstrate how to handle disagreements respectfully.

Chapter 6: Stress Management for Parents

Parenting is a fulfilling journey, but it's not without its share of stressors. In this chapter, we explore the critical relationship between stress and anger, and we delve into strategies and techniques for managing stress effectively as a parent.

The Connection Between Stress and Anger

The Stress-Anger Cycle: Stress and anger often go hand in hand. When we're under chronic stress, our tolerance for frustration diminishes, making us more prone to anger. On the flip side, anger itself can be a stressor, creating a vicious cycle.

Impact on Parenting: Stress can significantly impact your ability to parent effectively. It can lead to impatience, irritability, and reduced emotional resilience, all of which can contribute to anger.

Children's Sensitivity: Children are highly sensitive to their parents' stress levels. They can pick up on tension and may react to it with their own stress or challenging behaviors.

Stress-Reduction Techniques

Mindfulness Meditation: Mindfulness practices, such as meditation, can help you stay grounded and present in the moment. Regular mindfulness sessions can reduce stress and enhance your ability to respond calmly.

Physical Activity: Engaging in regular physical activity releases endorphins, which are natural stress relievers. Even a short daily walk or yoga session can have a positive impact.

Deep Breathing: Deep breathing exercises can instantly calm your nervous system. Practice slow, deep breaths when you feel stress building.

Journaling: Keeping a journal can provide an outlet for your thoughts and emotions. Write about your stressors and explore potential solutions.

Progressive Muscle Relaxation: This technique involves tensing and then releasing each muscle group in your body to reduce physical tension.

Time Management: Effective time management can reduce the stress associated with feeling overwhelmed. Prioritize tasks, set realistic goals, and learn to say no when necessary.

Social Support: Lean on your support network. Talking to friends or family members can provide emotional relief and perspective.

Prioritizing Self-Care

Regular Sleep: Prioritize quality sleep. Lack of sleep can amplify stress and diminish your ability to manage emotions effectively.

Healthy Eating: A balanced diet provides your body with the nutrients it needs to cope with stress. Avoid excessive caffeine and sugar, which can contribute to mood swings.

Me Time: Set aside time for yourself each day, even if it's just a few minutes. Engage in activities that bring you joy and relaxation.

Seek Professional Help: If stress becomes overwhelming or chronic, don't hesitate to seek help from a mental health professional. Therapy can provide valuable coping strategies.

Parenting Support Groups: Joining a parenting support group can connect you with others facing similar challenges. Sharing experiences and advice can be reassuring.

Limit Exposure to Stressors: Identify sources of stress in your life and explore ways to reduce or eliminate them. This may involve setting boundaries or making lifestyle changes.

Practice Self-Compassion: Be kind to yourself. Parenting is demanding, and it's okay to acknowledge your limitations and take breaks when needed.

Managing stress is not just a personal benefit; it's a gift to your family as well. By effectively managing stress, you enhance your ability to respond to the demands of parenting with patience and resilience. Your children benefit from a calmer, more emotionally available parent, and you create a healthier family environment. In the chapters that follow, we will continue to explore strategies for nurturing emotional well-being in yourself and your children.

Chapter 7: Parenting Under Pressure

Parenting is a rewarding journey, but it's not without its challenges, and sometimes these challenges come with added pressure. In this chapter, we'll explore various aspects of parenting under pressure, from balancing work and family life to coping with sleep deprivation and managing sibling rivalry when you're raising multiple children.

Balancing Work and Family

Parenting often goes hand in hand with careers and other responsibilities. Finding the right balance between work and family can be a significant challenge:

Time Management: Effective time management is key to balancing your responsibilities. Prioritize your tasks, set boundaries, and allocate quality time for your family.

Quality over Quantity: It's not always about the quantity of time you spend with your children, but the quality. Make the most of the time you have by being present and engaged.

Delegate and Seek Support: Don't hesitate to delegate tasks or seek support from a partner, family members, or childcare services. Building a support network can alleviate some of the pressure.

Self-Care: Remember to take care of yourself. Parenting is a demanding job, and self-care is essential for maintaining your physical and emotional well-being.

Coping with Sleep Deprivation

Sleep deprivation often accompanies the early years of parenting, but it can be a source of significant pressure. Here are some strategies to cope:

Establish a Routine: Create a consistent sleep routine for your child to encourage better sleep patterns.

Share Night Duties: If possible, share night duties with a partner or a trusted caregiver to ensure both parents get adequate rest.

Nap When You Can: Take advantage of nap times, both for your child and yourself. Short power naps can help you recharge.

Seek Support: Reach out to friends or family members who can provide relief and allow you to catch up on sleep.

Handling Sibling Rivalry and Parenting Multiple Children

If you have more than one child, managing sibling rivalry and parenting multiple children simultaneously can be challenging:

Individual Attention: Each child has unique needs. Make an effort to spend one-on-one time with each of your children to nurture their individual relationships with you.

Conflict Resolution: Teach your children conflict resolution skills from an early age. Encourage them to express their feelings and find peaceful solutions to disputes.

Fairness and Equality: Be mindful of treating your children fairly, rather than equally. Recognize and respect their individual strengths and challenges.

Teamwork and Bonding: Encourage a sense of teamwork among your children. Engage in activities that promote bonding and cooperation.

Seek Guidance: If sibling rivalry becomes overwhelming, consider seeking guidance from a parenting expert or counselor. They can provide strategies for managing conflicts.

Parenting under pressure is a reality for many families. It's important to remember that you're not alone in facing these challenges, and there are resources and support available to help you navigate them. By finding balance, managing sleep deprivation, and fostering healthy sibling relationships, you can reduce the pressure and enjoy the joys of parenthood to the fullest. In the chapters that follow, we'll continue to explore strategies for thriving as a parent and nurturing your child's well-being.

CHAPTER 8: TEACHING CHILDREN ABOUT ANGER

As parents, one of our responsibilities is to guide our children in understanding and managing their emotions, including anger. In this chapter, we'll explore various strategies for teaching children about anger, from age-appropriate discussions about emotions to modeling healthy expressions of anger and imparting essential conflict resolution skills.

Age-Appropriate Discussions About Emotions

Start Early: Begin discussing emotions with your child from an early age. Use simple language and age-appropriate terms to explain feelings like happiness, sadness, and anger.

Emotion Identification: Encourage your child to identify and label their emotions. Ask questions like, "How are you feeling right now?" and help them express their emotions through words.

Empathy Development: Teach your child to recognize emotions in others. When reading stories or observing real-life situations, ask questions like, "How do you think that person feels?"

Modeling Healthy Expression of Anger

Lead by Example: Children learn by observing their parents. Model healthy expressions of anger by calmly discussing your own emotions and demonstrating problem-solving skills.

Anger Is Natural: Normalize anger as a natural emotion. Let your child know that everyone gets angry at times, and it's okay to feel that way.

Practice Patience: Show your child how to manage frustration and anger through patience and self-regulation. Explain that taking a deep breath or counting to ten can help calm angry feelings.

Avoid Aggressive Behavior: Ensure your child witnesses healthy expressions of anger. Avoid yelling, shouting, or physical aggression when you're upset.

Teaching Conflict Resolution Skills

Active Listening: Teach your child the importance of listening actively when others express their anger. Encourage them to pay attention to the speaker and ask questions for clarification.

Use "I" Statements: Show your child how to express their feelings using "I" statements. For instance, instead of saying, "You made me mad," they can say, "I felt upset when..."

Empathy and Perspective-Taking: Help your child understand the feelings and perspectives of others involved in a conflict. Discuss how different people can have different viewpoints.

Apologizing and Forgiving: Explain the importance of apologizing when they have wronged someone and forgiving when they have been wronged. Model these behaviors in your own interactions.

Cooling-Off Periods: Teach your child to recognize when they need a break to cool off during a conflict. Encourage them to revisit the issue once both parties have calmed down.

Teaching children about anger is a valuable life skill. By fostering open discussions about emotions, modeling healthy anger expressions, and imparting conflict resolution skills, you empower your child to understand, manage, and use anger constructively.

Chapter 9: Building Positive Parent-Child Relationships

A strong and positive parent-child relationship forms the foundation for healthy emotional development in children. In this chapter, we explore key strategies for strengthening these bonds through quality time, parenting with empathy and compassion, and rebuilding trust after anger outbursts.

Strengthening Bonds Through Quality Time

Unplugged Quality Time: Set aside dedicated, technology-free time to engage with your child. This could be playing games, reading together, or simply having a heartfelt conversation.

Shared Interests: Discover and participate in activities that your child enjoys. Shared interests can create lasting memories and strengthen your connection.

Active Listening: When your child speaks, practice active listening. Give them your full attention, make eye contact, and ask open-ended questions to encourage them to express themselves.

Family Traditions: Establishing family traditions, whether it's a weekly movie night or a monthly outing, can provide opportunities for bonding and create a sense of belonging.

Express Affection: Don't hesitate to show physical affection through hugs, kisses, and reassuring pats on the back. Verbal expressions of love and affirmation are also essential.

Parenting with Empathy and Compassion

Understanding Their Perspective: Put yourself in your child's shoes and strive to understand their perspective. This fosters empathy and allows you to respond to their needs more effectively.

Acknowledge Feelings: When your child expresses their emotions, acknowledge their feelings without judgment. Phrases like "I see you're upset" convey empathy and support.

Stay Calm and Patient: Parenting can be challenging, and children may test your patience. Remember to remain calm and patient, even in the face of difficult moments.

Validating Emotions: Let your child know that their feelings are valid. Avoid dismissing their emotions with statements like "You shouldn't feel that way."

Problem-Solving Together: When conflicts arise, involve your child in problem-solving. This teaches them valuable skills and shows that their input is valued.

Rebuilding Trust After Anger Outbursts

Apologize Sincerely: If you've had an anger outburst that hurt your child, apologize sincerely. Acknowledge your mistake and express your commitment to doing better.

Use the Experience as a Learning Opportunity: Talk to your child about what happened and why it upset you. Help them understand that everyone makes mistakes, and it's an opportunity for growth.

Set a Positive Example: Model healthy ways of managing anger and frustration. Show your child that it's okay to acknowledge your emotions and find constructive ways to address them.

Implement Strategies: Discuss strategies you can both use when anger flares. This might include taking deep breaths, using time-outs, or practicing mindfulness exercises.

Rebuild Trust Over Time: Rebuilding trust takes time, and it involves consistent, positive interactions. Continue to nurture your relationship with your child through love and support.

Building a positive parent-child relationship is an ongoing journey that requires effort, patience, and a commitment to understanding and nurturing your child's emotional needs. By dedicating quality time, parenting with empathy and compassion, and addressing anger outbursts with honesty and care, you can create a strong and enduring bond that will benefit both you and your child throughout their life. In the chapters that follow, we'll explore further ways to navigate the complexities of parenthood and promote emotional well-being in your family.

Chapter 10: Seeking Support and Professional Help

Parenting is a journey filled with ups and downs, and there may come a time when you need extra support or professional help. In this chapter, we'll explore the importance of recognizing when to seek help.

Recognizing When to Seek Help

Persistent Challenges: If you find that you're facing persistent challenges in parenting, such as ongoing behavioral issues with your child or frequent conflicts, it may be a sign that it's time to seek help.

Emotional Strain: Parenting can be emotionally demanding, and it's natural to experience stress and frustration. However, if you're consistently overwhelmed or struggling to cope with your emotions, it's a signal that you should seek support.

Impact on Daily Life: When parenting challenges begin to affect your daily life, relationships, or work, it's a clear indication that external assistance may be beneficial.

Child's Well-being: Always prioritize your child's well-being. If you believe that your child's emotional or psychological health is at risk, seeking help becomes imperative.

Support Groups for Parents

Online and In-Person Groups: Parenting support groups come in various forms, including online forums, local community groups, and organized meetings. These groups provide a space for parents to share experiences and advice.

Shared Experiences: Support groups allow you to connect with other parents who may be going through similar challenges. Sharing experiences can be comforting and reassuring.

Learning Opportunities: In addition to emotional support, parenting groups often provide valuable information and resources on topics related to child development and effective parenting strategies.

Reduced Isolation: Parenting can sometimes feel isolating, especially if you're facing unique challenges. Joining a support group can alleviate this isolation and provide a sense of belonging.

Therapy and Counseling Options

Individual Therapy: Individual therapy provides a one-on-one setting where you can explore your thoughts, emotions, and challenges with a trained therapist. It can help you gain insight into your parenting style and develop coping strategies.

Family Therapy: Family therapy involves sessions with both parents and children. It's particularly beneficial when there are family dynamics or conflicts that need to be addressed.

Parenting Classes: Parenting classes offer structured learning and guidance on effective parenting techniques. They can help you acquire new skills and strategies.

Counseling for Children: If your child is facing emotional or behavioral challenges, consider counseling for them. A qualified child therapist can work with your child to address specific issues.

Couples Counseling: Parenting can strain relationships. Couples counseling can help you and your partner navigate conflicts and strengthen your partnership.

Chapter 11: Maintaining Progress and Preventing Relapse

Your journey toward effective anger management and positive parenting doesn't end when you've made initial progress. In this chapter, we'll explore the importance of staying committed to change, strategies for long-term anger management, and how to handle setbacks and prevent relapses.

Staying Committed to Change

Mindful Self-Reflection: Continue to engage in mindful self-reflection. Regularly assess your anger management strategies and parenting techniques to ensure they align with your goals.

Setting Realistic Expectations: Be realistic about the challenges of parenting and anger management. Understand that setbacks may occur, but they don't negate the progress you've made.

Consistency: Consistency is key in parenting and anger management. Stay committed to the strategies and techniques that have been effective for you and your family.

Seeking Support: Don't hesitate to seek support when you need it. Whether it's from a therapist, support group, or trusted friend, reaching out can provide the encouragement and guidance you require.

Strategies for Long-Term Anger Management

Continual Learning: Parenting and anger management are ongoing learning processes. Stay informed about new research and techniques in both fields to enhance your skills.

Emotional Regulation: Continue to practice emotional regulation techniques. Regularly engage in activities that help you stay emotionally balanced, such as mindfulness exercises or relaxation techniques.

Stress Management: Stress is a common trigger for anger. Maintain a robust stress management routine, incorporating activities like exercise, relaxation, and time for self-care.

Effective Communication: Keep working on your communication skills, both with your child and your partner. Effective communication is a cornerstone of positive parenting.

Problem-Solving: Encourage and practice problem-solving as a family. Teach your child the importance of finding constructive solutions to conflicts.

Handling Setbacks and Relapses

Acknowledge Setbacks: Setbacks are a natural part of any journey toward change. Acknowledge them without judgment and view them as opportunities for growth.

Learn from Mistakes: Analyze setbacks to understand their underlying causes. What triggered the relapse, and how can you avoid a similar situation in the future?

Revisit Strategies: When you experience a setback, revisit the anger management and parenting strategies that have been effective in the past. Implement them consistently.

Seek Professional Help: If setbacks become persistent or severe, consider seeking professional help. A therapist can provide guidance and support during challenging times.

Self-Compassion: Practice self-compassion during setbacks. Understand that you're human, and making mistakes is part of the learning process. Treat yourself with kindness and forgiveness.

Family Dialogue: Engage in open and honest dialogue with your family about the setback. Explain what happened and express your commitment to positive change.

Maintaining progress and preventing relapse require ongoing dedication and self-awareness. By staying committed to your journey, continually learning and implementing effective strategies, and handling setbacks with resilience and self-compassion, you can create a lasting foundation for healthy anger management and positive parenting. Remember that growth is a lifelong process, and the effort you put into it benefits both you and your child. In the chapters that follow, we'll explore further aspects of parenting and emotional well-being for your family.

CHAPTER 12: SUSTAINING GROWTH AS A PARENT

In this final chapter of our book, we delve into the importance of sustaining growth as a parent. Parenthood is an ongoing journey, and even as we reach the end of this book, we must remember that our role as parents continues to evolve. Sustaining growth means continually adapting to the changing needs of our children and ourselves.

The Dynamic Nature of Parenting

Parenting is not a static experience but a dynamic one. Just as our children grow and develop, so do we as parents. Our strategies, techniques, and understanding of parenting evolve over time.

Recognizing this dynamic nature is the first step toward sustaining growth.

As parents, we must embrace the fact that our children are not the only ones who change; we do too. Our journey as parents involves continuous learning and adaptation. What worked in the early years may need adjustments as our children become teenagers, and our approaches may evolve further as they transition into young adults.

The dynamic nature of parenting is a reminder that growth is an integral part of the process. It's not about achieving a perfect parenting style but about being open to change and learning from our experiences.

Lifelong Learning

A commitment to lifelong learning is at the heart of sustaining growth as a parent. The world is constantly changing, and so are the challenges that our children face. To meet these challenges, we must remain curious, open-minded, and receptive to new ideas and perspectives.

Learning can take many forms. It can involve reading books and articles on parenting, attending workshops or seminars, or engaging in discussions with other parents. It can also be a simple act of seeking feedback from our children and being open to their insights.

The willingness to learn and adapt not only benefits us but also sets a positive example for our children.

They see that growth is a lifelong process, and they learn the value of curiosity and resilience.

Connecting with Your Child

As your child grows, their needs and interests will change. Sustaining growth as a parent means staying connected with your child by actively engaging in their world. This might involve exploring their hobbies, discussing their interests, and being a consistent presence in their lives.

Connection goes beyond physical presence; it's about emotional availability. It's about being a parent who listens without judgment, who offers support and encouragement, and who creates a safe space for your child to share their thoughts and feelings.

Conclusion

As we conclude our journey through "Anger Management for Parents," we want to express our deep appreciation for your commitment and dedication to becoming the best parent you can be. Parenthood is an ever-evolving adventure, and your willingness to explore the intricacies of managing anger and nurturing emotional health sets a remarkable example.

Embrace imperfections, for they are the threads that weave your unique parenting journey. Recognize that growth, not perfection, is the goal. Celebrate your progress, no matter how small, as each step is a victory.

You are inspiring the future. Your love, lessons, and memories will shape your child's life profoundly. You are their role model, protector, and cheerleader. Your influence is immeasurable.

Lastly, thank you for trusting us on this journey. Your dedication inspires us, and we are grateful to have been a part of your support system.

In the adventure of parenthood, hold fast to your commitment, and continue inspiring with unwavering love. Your journey is a legacy, a testament to the power of love and the resilience of the human spirit. May your days be filled with laughter, your hearts with love, and your future with boundless possibilities.

Milton Keynes UK
Ingram Content Group UK Ltd.
UKHW020923201123
432908UK00021B/3241

9 798868 983078